First Facts®

Christmas around the World

Christmas in
SWEDEN

by Cheryl L. Enderlein

CAPSTONE PRESS
a capstone imprint

First Facts are published by Capstone Press,
1710 Roe Crest Drive, North Mankato, Minnesota 56003
www.capstonepub.com

Library of Congress Cataloging-in-Publication Data
Enderlein, Cheryl L.
Christmas in Sweden / by Cheryl L. Enderlein.
p. cm. —(First facts. Christmas around the world)
Includes bibliographical references and index.
Summary: "Describes the customs, songs, foods, and activities associated with the celebration of
Christmas in Sweden"—Provided by publisher.
ISBN 978-1-62065-140-7 (library binding)
ISBN 978-1-4765-1062-0 (eBook PDF)
1. Christmas—Sweden—Juvenile literature. 2. Sweden—Social life and customs—Juvenile literature.
I. Title.

GT4987.6.E63 2013
394.266309485—dc23   2012026284

Editorial Credits
Christine Peterson, editor; Ted Williams, designer; Eric Gohl, media researcher; Kathy McColley,
production specialist

Photo Credits
Alamy: Catchlight Visual Services, 8, Chad Ehlers, 16; Capstone Studio: Karon Dubke, 21;
Dreamstime: Barbro Rutgersson, 18; Fotolia: Gerhard Seybert, 5; Getty Images: Gamma-Rapho/
Frederic Reglain, 15; iStockphotos: Cindy England, 12; Newscom: Getty Images/AFP/Jonathan
Nackstrand, cover, 11, Zuma Press/Rob Schoenbaum, 1; Shutterstock: Cio, 7

Design Elements: Shutterstock

Printed in China
122014   008687R

TABLE OF CONTENTS

Christmas in Sweden

Winter in Sweden can be cold and dark. But during Christmas, lights, decorations, and music brighten up the countryside. Christmas is December 25. But in Sweden, people celebrate Christmas for more than one day. Holiday celebrations begin four weeks before Christmas, during **Advent**. They end on January 13, Saint Knut's Day.

Advent—the season beginning four Sundays before Christmas

How to Say It!

In Sweden, people say *"God Jul,"* which means "Good Christmas."

Sweden

5

The First Christmas

On Christmas, **Christians** around the world celebrate the birth of **Jesus**. Long ago, Mary and Joseph went to the town of Bethlehem. Mary was going to have a baby. But when the couple got to Bethlehem, the town was crowded. Mary and Joseph had no place to stay. So they spent the night in a stable. There, Jesus was born.

Christian—a person who follows a religion based on the teachings of Jesus
Jesus—the founder of the Christian religion

7

Christmas Symbols

Christians believe a bright star appeared the night Jesus was born. Three Kings followed the star to find Jesus in Bethlehem. Today Swedish people hang Advent stars in their windows at Christmas. These decorations remind people of the star the Three Kings followed.

People also light Advent candles to mark the weeks before Christmas. One candle is lit on each of the four Sundays of Advent.

Christmas Celebrations

A crown of candles marks the Saint Lucia Day celebration on December 13. On this day Swedish people honor Saint Lucia. This Christian girl lived long ago and helped people in need. Saint Lucia's crown brings light into a dark world.

On Saint Lucia Day, a family's oldest daughter gets up before sunrise. She puts on a long white dress with a red sash. She wears a crown made of lighted candles. She then takes food to her family.

CHRISTMAS FACT!

Some Swedish people believe the straw goat will protect them from harm.

Christmas Decorations

Straw **ornaments** decorate homes and trees in Sweden during Christmas. The straw reminds people that Jesus was born in a stable. Swedish children make straw ornaments in shapes of stars, animals, and angels. A straw goat often guards the Christmas tree.

Heart-shaped baskets are also popular. People fill the baskets with candy or small gifts. They hang the baskets on their trees.

ornament—a small, attractive object used for decoration

Santa Claus

In Sweden Santa doesn't bring holiday gifts. Instead, *Jultomten* (yool-TAWM-ten) brings presents to good girls and boys. Jultomten looks like Santa. He has a white beard and wears a long red coat. But Jultomten comes during the day. Children watch for him from their windows. He knocks on doors, asking if there are good children inside.

CHRISTMAS FACT!

Some believe Jultomten is an elf who hides under the floor or stairs.

Some gift tags have poems. The poems give clues about what present is inside.

Christmas Presents

In Sweden people exchange gifts on Christmas Eve. Gifts are called *julklappar* (yool-KLP-pur). The name comes from an old **tradition**. Years ago people would leave gifts outside doors. They would then knock on the doors and run away.

Today Jultomten often hands gifts to children. He reads a tag on each gift. The tag tells who will get the gift.

tradition—a custom, idea, or belief passed down through time

Christmas Food

Christmas cookies are tasty holiday treats. In Sweden a popular cookie is *pepparkakor* (PEH-pahr-kaa-koor). These cookies taste like gingerbread. They are shaped like hearts, stars, and goats.

On Christmas Eve families gather for a large meal of meats, dried fish, potatoes, and other foods. For dessert people enjoy sweet rice pudding. The pudding often has an almond hidden inside. It is believed that whoever finds the almond will marry in the coming year.

CHRISTMAS FACT!

On Christmas Eve people may dip bread into thin soup. This act reminds people of a time when food was hard to find.

Christmas Songs

Christmas carols are a popular part of Swedish holiday celebrations. On Christmas Eve, families sing carols and dance around the tree. Carols are also sung during Christmas church services.

On January 6, Star Boys walk the streets and sing during the **Epiphany**. Holiday celebrations end on Saint Knut's Day, which is January 13. People have parties and sing as they take down their Christmas trees.

Epiphany—a Christian festival celebrated January 6 to mark the Three Kings' visit to baby Jesus

Hands-On:
MAKE A HEART-SHAPED BASKET

Decorate your tree like kids in Sweden with these heart-shaped baskets. You can fill the baskets with candy or other holiday treats.

What You Need
- **drinking glass**
- **red paper**
- **pencil**
- **white paper**
- **scissors**
- **glue**
- **ribbon**

What You Do
1. Place the glass on a piece of red paper. Use a pencil to trace around the glass to make a circle. Repeat with the white paper.
2. Use a scissors to cut out both circles. Fold the circles in half.
3. Tuck the white circle inside the red circle so the bottoms touch. The folded circles will now form a heart. Glue the sides together
4. Cut a 5-inch (13-centimeter) piece of ribbon.
5. Glue one end of the ribbon to the middle of one side. Repeat on the other side. Be careful not to glue the basket shut.
6. When dry, fill the basket with treats, and hang it on your tree.

GLOSSARY

Advent (AD-vent)—the season beginning four Sundays before Christmas

Christian (KRIS-chuhn)—a person who follows a religion based on the teachings of Jesus

Epiphany (ih-PIF-uh-nee)—a Christian festival celebrated on January 6 to mark the Three Kings' visit to baby Jesus

Jesus (JEE-zuhs)—the founder of the Christian religion

ornament (OR-nuh-muhnt)—a small, attractive object used for decoration

tradition (truh-DISH-uhn)—a custom, idea, or belief passed down through time

READ MORE

Hyde, Katherine Bolger. *Lucia, Saint of Light.* Ben Lomond, Calif.: Conciliar Press, 2009.

Koestler-Grack, Rachel A. *Sweden.* Exploring Countries. Minneapolis: Bellwether Media, 2011.

Trunkhill, Brenda. *Christmas around the World.* St. Louis: Concordia Publishing House, 2009.

INTERNET SITES

FactHound offers a safe, fun way to find Internet sites related to this book. All of the sites on FactHound have been researched by our staff.

Here's all you do:

Visit *www.facthound.com*

Type in this code: 9781620651407

INDEX